CLOISTER

BOOKS

Cloister Books are inspired by the monastic custom of reading as one walks slowly in the monastery cloister— a place of silence, centering, and calm. Within these pages you will find a similar space in which to pray and reflect on the presence of God.

The Shattering Sound of Amazing Grace

The Shattering Sound of Amazing Grace

Disquieting Tales from Saint John's Gospel

David J. Schlafer

Cowley Publications
CAMBRIDGE, MASSACHUSETTS

Library of Congress Cataloging-in-Publication Data
Schlafer, David J., 1944–
   The shattering sound of Amazing grace : disquieting tales from Saint John's Gospel / David J. Schlafer.
       p.   cm.
   Includes bibliographical references.
   ISBN 10: 1-56101-247-5 ISBN-13: 978-1-56101-247-3 (pbk. : alk. paper)
1. Bible. N.T. John—Meditations.   2. Amazing grace (Hymn)   I. Title.
   BS2615.54.S35   2006
   226.5'06—dc22

                                                        2005036024

Unless indicated otherwise, scripture quotations are taken from The New Revised Standard Version of the Bible, © 1989, by the Division of Christian Education of the National Council of the Churches of Christ in the United States of America. Used by permission.

Cover painting: Charles Perkalis
Cover design: Brad Norr Design
Interior design: Wendy Holdman

This book was printed in the United States of America on acid-free paper.

Cowley Publications
4 Brattle Street
Cambridge, Massachusetts 02138
800-225-1534 • www.cowley.org

Every idea of God we form,
God must, in mercy, shatter.

—C. S. Lewis
(*Letters to Malcolm—
Chiefly on Prayer*)

Contents

Amazing grace! How sweet the sound that
     saved a wretch like me.
I once was lost, but now am found; was blind,
     but now I see.

'Twas grace that taught my heart to fear, and
     grace my fears relieved.
How precious did that grace appear the hour
     I first believed.

The Lord has promised good to me, his word
     my hope secures.
He will my shield and portion be as long as
     life endures.

Through many dangers, toils, and snares
     I have already come.
'Tis grace has brought me safe thus far,
     and grace will lead me home.

When we've been there ten thousand years,
     bright shining as the sun,
We've no less days to sing God's praise than
     when we'd first begun.

Acknowledgements and Dedication

During weekdays in Lent, St. Paul's Episcopal Church, Richmond, Virginia, sustains an extraordinary tradition—noonday prayer and sermon, both preceded and followed by as sumptuous a Lenten luncheon as the season will allow.

Volunteers from parish and community prepare and serve the food, proceeds from the sale of which go toward the support of local charities. Government workers stroll over from the state capitol just down the street, and are joined by employees from downtown businesses, local residents, passersby, and parishioners who drive into town from surrounding suburbs for the event.

Some folks come early (so as to eat and pray), some come late (so as to pray and eat). Some just come and eat. The food is so good, however, that practically no one comes just to pray. Nobody eats twice, of course—it is Lent, after all.

Guest preachers are invited to offer a week-long series of meditations—five brief sermons, fifteen minutes, max. The preacher of the week also spends an evening with interested parishioners, sharing food, fellowship, and informal but focused conversation—a multi-dimensional feast for all involved.

Through the kindness of *The Rev. Dr. Hilary B. Smith,* friend and former preaching student, then Associate Rector, and *The Rev. Canon Robert B. Hetherington,* Rector, I was given this preaching privilege at St. Paul's during a year in which the theme for the Lenten series was "Amazing Grace, How Sweet the Sound." The meditations first given there have "grown up" into this Cloister Book.

I salute St. Paul's for its vision, give thanks to Hilary for fostering the invitation, and gratefully recognize Bob and his gracious co-workers who lavished upon me an outpouring akin to what the author of the Fourth Gospel describes as "grace upon grace."

I am grateful beyond measure for such grace that has come to me from others as well:

 ～ *The Rev. Susan Thon Burns,* Rector of The Church of the Redeemer, who preached the sermon referenced in the final meditation— and, much more importantly, is my treasured colleague in ordained ministry at this loving parish of which I am a member.

in the chronology of the storyteller). Into both settings Jesus strides. Surveying the situation quickly, he makes a deft, decisive move. He disrupts the predictable flow ("After X, comes Y—everybody knows that!"). Jesus sharply jolts the rhythms of interaction-as-usual. Then off he goes, picking up no pieces, making no move to deal with the dust his actions have kicked up as he sweeps across center stage. Jesus is there and gone—but not before he has reshaped the contour of events. Yet, in so curious a fashion!

ﻌ

John designates the one hundred eighty or so gratuitous gallons of the finest wine as a sign by which Jesus "revealed his glory." What did we miss? Where did the "miracle" happen? When? This significant wedding guest seems to be taking pains to remain inconspicuous. He ducks his own mother's attempt to set him up for recognition (then turns around and does what he has just declined to do). He gets other guys to do the heavy lifting (filling thirty-gallon water jugs is no small task—especially without accessible pipes and water faucets). He lets the chief steward announce the groom's sudden reversal of fortunes (thereby seriously jeopardizing the poor fellow's credentials as custodian-in-charge of festival libations). There is no photo op, no image of Jesus, hands over stone jars, smiling for the camera, accepting adulation for services rendered, capitalizing on the political potential inherent in the moment ("If we can make wine out of water, imagine what we can do about the weapons of mass destruction wielded by Roman pagans!").

Nothing noticeable has changed after water becomes wine—save that his close colleagues are impressed enough that they "believe" (whatever that might mean at this point in the story). This "sign" does not appear to have accomplished anything.

But maybe our focus is misplaced. Perhaps, rather than look at Jesus, we should look at everybody else. And rather than scrutinizing the details of the immediate event, we should try to trace its trajectories toward the horizon.

The newlyweds, the bride and groom whose wedding feast has been deluged with fine free wine poured into the very heart of it—what do they do? What will be *their* next move?

- Will they simply shake their heads in delighted disbelief? ("We really lucked out! Somebody must be looking after us! But, then, we certainly are a deserving couple, are we not?")
- Might the sudden wine infusion prevent a gathering nuptial squall? ("What's wrong

with your family if they've let the wine run out?" "Well, they can hardly be held responsible for knowing that thirteen extra folks would show up, now can they?")

~ If there is a storm brewing, will Jesus' inconspicuous interruption serve as a catalyst in altering the weather? Will they forgive whoever was responsible for, or utterly incapable of preventing, so egregious a social error?

~ Will they ever afterward, though grateful for escaping embarrassment in the nick of time, be very meticulous about their strategic planning, each ever so guarded about their behaviors (and each other's)? Will they live their whole lives looking at everything and everyone with suspicious, furrowed brows?

~ Will they, perhaps, take the gift for granted, as a matter of right, saving every last gallon, never sharing a drop? ("After all, we never know when we might run out of wine again! Miracles don't knock twice!")

~ Or upon being overwhelmed from out of nowhere with rivers of excellent wine, will gratitude gush forth from bride and groom, greening a gracious, fruitful marriage? ("What a gift we were given! What a difference it made! Whom do we know or see that could use some refreshment we could share?")

Open questions, all of these—"what if's" on the far side of an encounter with Amazing Grace. We don't know what the answer is (I suspect the Gospel author knows full well how little good it would do the reader if he provided it). But that each and both—husband and wife—must make an answer to such questions is beyond doubt. What would you and I do if we had been thus graced? What have we done when we have been in such a place? When love is poured out upon us, do we drink it deeply and with gratitude, or sip it languidly with jaded palates?

The couple, of course, might not themselves have even known that the wine had run out. Everyone else may have been scrambling to keep them from knowing, saving them, as long as possible, from embarrassment. But all the other players in the drama have in one way or another been affected by Jesus' intervention also; how they respond will also make a difference.

       ◦ Does Jesus' mother become outraged because she seems to have been upstaged? Or is she able to recognize, with satisfaction and delight, that she has played a significant role, even though she, like her strange-talking son, gets no credit?

~ The servants also have had a role in making possible the difference that Jesus somehow catalyzes. Is it, for them, simply all in a day's work? Will they regard themselves as being used? Or, being the ones in the situation who are least influential but most in the know (except for Jesus' companions), will they, thereafter, regard their own work with different eyes (though everyone else sees them only as servants)?

~ What about the poor chief steward? How many times has he done such honors before, always presiding in the same efficient way at the same ceremony? What will the taste of wine do for his palate? For his understanding of his role and vocation?

~ Where are you and I in relation to the various players in this drama? Perhaps, like the disciples, we "believe." What does such belief entail? How have we reacted when we find ourselves operating in roles analogous to each of these players? What do we do when Grace makes a subtle, unobtrusive entry—but then requires us, confronted with gift, to decide how we will share in the celebration?

✑

How different the subsequent scene at the temple! The Jesus who, at Cana, is completely unobtrusive with respect to the ceremonies, now brings them crashing down. What an upsetting day for all concerned—temple officials, currency exchange agents, those who trade one kind of coin for another so that they can purchase and present unblemished sacrifices! Jesus turns the tables on all of them. Predictable patterns of exchange are interrupted, challenged, dismantled. (It is possible that what Jesus intends is the restoration of traditions recently set aside by Caiaphas. "But we've *always* done it that way" is often the protest when the system in place was instituted only recently.)

The system as it stands has a logic of its own—one well tuned to the givens of the day:

- The need for sacrifices well pleasing to God, representing primacy and totality of commitment on the part of those whom God has chosen as Covenant People
- The difficulty of ensuring the quality of such sacrifices, since they are often brought from a long distance over rugged terrain

- The need to "just say NO" to the idolatrous symbols of a repressive pagan regime
- The difficulty of making such a clear repudiation in a way that is not suicidal

How does one enact honor to God, Owner and Giver of All, without incurring inordinate expense at least—perhaps inevitable bloodshed as well? This is a rational, religiously responsible systemic answer to such difficult questions. And Jesus summarily upends it. "The Cleansing of the Temple" is how his action is often designated. But what needs "cleaning up" would seem to be the chaos Jesus leaves in his own wake as he charges through the courtyard, driving out sheep and cattle, sending rolls of coins flying in all directions.

His stated objection is that the temple has become a marketplace. Why is that a problem? Worship, too, is an exchange—one involving tangible as well as intangible goods and services. Perhaps, however unconsciously, over time one kind of exchange has begun to stand for another—or that which has been rightly understood as a means to an end has inched, by degrees, toward becoming an end in itself. Prayers and ceremonies offered for their own sake, rather than as ways of connecting with God and with one another.

If that is so, then this chaotic shakeup might be

a wake-up call for those involved—a vivid invitation to consider the meaning of what is being traded back and forth. Perhaps religion is in peril whenever (even if for good reason) it is conducted as though it were business as usual.

Systems by which sacramental interchanges are celebrated have a certain inertia about them. Those who interrupt them, suggesting not just different liturgies, but different ways of understanding the same liturgies (which is even more unsettling) are seldom welcome in the courtyard. There is always a tendency to try to package Grace, however amazing it may have seemed when first set loose, and then market it in exchange for a fixed price.

Once again—what will all of this come to mean for the various players involved? In their respective ways, will they simply pick up all the pieces and paste them back together? Hire security guards to protect themselves against the future incursions of such temple terrorists? Or might the whole upsetting affair remain in their awareness as at best a frightening confusion, at worst a deeply offending sacrilege; until a day long hence, on the other side of an empty tomb, when it clicks into place, quietly catalytic, as a retrospective epiphany?

What about disciples, then and there, here and now, on a steep learning curve as to what in the world *Incarnation* means? What about those of us who take in both of these events—fresh wine pouring from religious ceremonial purification jars, and religious ceremonial infrastructure disintegrating in cacophony—one event hard upon the other?

"Signs," the Evangelist designates these strange early events on Jesus' social calendar. Mixed signals, surely! One is so subtle, nobody even sees it happen; the other is pretty hard for anyone in sight to miss. One seems a compassionate and generous sign, the other harsh and provocative. The sign of abundant wine, to our eyes anyway, looks like an *ad hoc,* one-time favor, a family affair; the sign of upended temple courtyard tables carries community implications with relevance for other times and places.

Where is the grace in all of this? Is Jesus, in these two signs, sending contradictory signals? Or could they be complementary, converging—and if so, how?

Maybe there is a congruent modus operandi here: disarrange the order of business as usual, not so much to make a point as to make a space for new possibilities that could make a world of difference.

However imaginatively we may dance with these two dramas of Amazing Grace, the one conclusion for which we have no license, artistic or theological, is that "they all lived happily ever after."

"Take that—now deal with it. I've made my move, now you make yours."

This sounds to me more in line with what Jesus' actions seem to say. He kicks the line of action onto a different trajectory, and then returns the steering wheel to those who were driving before.

‿℮

> Amazing grace! How sweet the sound that
>   saved a wretch like me.
> I once was lost, but now am found; was blind,
>   but now I see.

When I lift the familiar words from the Sunday evening evangelistic services of my childhood and sing them in the setting of Saint John's Gospel, the sweet sound of Amazing Grace has an altogether different flavor.

A wretch like me

This need not be a poor soul obsessed with anxious guilt feelings over grade school peccadilloes. People can be "wretched" in all sorts of ways—some having nothing to do with guilt—real or concocted. People can be trapped in social and religious structures—incapable even of sensing, let alone changing them. Some of the most wretched folks around are those who are being run over by the system. Others are wretched in a different way—victims of their own success as system managers. There can be profound poverty, whether you are on the downside or the upside of "just the way things are."

I once was lost, but now I'm found

Being "lost" can mean a host of things in addition to "not yet having accepted Jesus Christ as your personal savior." And there are more ways of being "found" than coming down the aisle to make a "decision for Christ"—though neither of these connotations is necessarily precluded. One can lose one's way on the landscape of the heart—one can be cut off, in many ways and for many reasons, from a life-giving relationship of mutual love and trust, or of meaningful achievement. ("He seems positively lost without her." "Since her novel was rejected, she seems to have lost all sense of purpose.") Being "found" might not entail a cozy feeling akin to a cup of hot cocoa in front of a fire after having been rescued from the midst of a winter blizzard. It might mean being centered, compass-oriented while still in the midst of the raging storm. Being found might consist of a continually deepening awareness of the necessity of one's call—even while under continual attacks of withering criticism, utterly alienated from those whom one had heretofore totally relied on as trusted friends.

'Twas blind, but now I see

Blindness brought to sight can happen in ways other than saying yes to the urgings of a persistent, well-intentioned "witness" who is trying to impress upon me the gravity of my sin and the urgent importance of my accepting God's all-pardoning love. I can be blinded by my own idealism, by my most deeply held moral convictions, by the genuine insights of good people whom I deeply trust. I can be blinded by the fixing focus of my healthiest passion. I can be blinded by my earnest attempts to impose sight upon another ("If only they could see it my way—God's way!"). I can be blind to alternative routes offered by those whom I find threatening and regard instinctively as competitors.

The grace of physical blindness is that its effects are evident to all and can be creatively compensated for. What Amazing Grace it takes to shed light on a kind of darkness in which I can wander, utterly unaware of what I am not seeing, defensively assuring myself and others, "My vision is just fine!"

"Seeing" might mean something other than feeling certain and voicing one's certitude in expected, pre-packaged phrases. It might mean becoming aware of the penumbra—the dim, barely visible shadows at the edges of former spotlight clarities—indicating that the more you see, the more you become aware of what you haven't a fix on (or even a clue about). Maybe seeing is a dawning sense of all you have never seen.

~e

In light of such a re-singing, let's briefly revisit some of the principals at the wedding feast and in the temple courts.

The bridal couple: Without the requisite amount of wine in a ceremonial setting on a high occasion, that newly formed family unit might well themselves be seriously "lost," off to a shaky start in the setting of their community. The problem with being lost, alone, is that once (and so easily) the process of alienation is set in motion, its momentum picks up speed—often the best efforts of those on either side of the widening chasm to the contrary. The chasm soon becomes impossible to breach unless someone somehow enters the situation and makes a difference, constructs some sort of bridging event—a counter-catalyst to the inexorable chain reaction of social chemistry.

"What an odd fellow you are! Most folks don't save

the best wine till last—but, hey, there it is, let's drink! Your health, and that of your bride!"

They can lose it again, surely, this newly married couple, in any number of ways. But at least on this, the occasion of their wedding feast, they are "found," by grace, in the company of their companions—gifted through the presence of one who is True Vine.

Can the couple, I wonder, in the midst of future occasions of awkwardness, be as resourcefully hospitable to others who, for whatever reason, seem lacking in what it takes to enter and foster communal celebration? Can they catch and convey the sweet sound and taste of Amazing Grace that has come so amazingly to them?

Analogous questions can be asked about the servants, the steward, the mother of Jesus, and especially the disciples for whom the "sign" signals something significant, though still opaque, about the identity of the One they have only recently encountered, and whom they are just taking first steps to follow. What do you do when Amazing Grace is interjected?

The money changers, the animal sellers, the animal buyers, the temple officials: Must we impose indignant blame on any of them? My first visit to Washington National Cathedral brought me through the great doors into pandemoniac preparations for a diocesan convention—complete with banquet tables set up right under the great stone lectern and pulpit. Ten seconds after I entered the sanctuary, a waiter dropped the lid of a fifty-gallon coffee urn on the stone floor. It made a less-than-quiet landing, and went rolling off under the banquet tables. Instinctively I found myself looking around the room for a man with a whip of cords. How dare they desecrate this Holy Space so cavalierly?

But let's not blame the animal sellers and the money changers like I spontaneously did. In every age they've got a job to do. There can be holiness in sitting down to supper in the midst of Holy Space. Formalized in liturgy, we call it Eucharist. What is necessarily wrong, occasionally at least, in orchestrating a more sensorily expansive symbol of the Messianic Banquet? Doing Church business is not necessarily profane just because it's business!

To draw the closest parallel, how would we react if Jesus entered our church at the administration of Communion and upended the chalice and the paten?

And yet, there are things that religious ecclesiocracies lose sight of sooner or later—even when they are surrounded by symbols designated as "sacred." One possible advantage emerging from the rude interruption of seemingly essential religious liturgies and infrastructures (whoever holds the whip hand) is the possibility of seeing how fragile they always are, and how brittle they can become when we cling to them.

"I once was blind, but now I see." Yes, indeed! But recognition of one's blindness often (perhaps only) comes in retrospect. (Storyteller John will have a thing or two to say on that score when he gets his narrative up and running, along about chapter 9.)

Could we conjecture that all those gathered in the temple courts were offered something quite different from, and altogether analogous to, what the initially wine-lacking wedding couple and their guests received: a good stiff dose of Amazing Grace, though none of them may have fully sensed the sweetness of it in the moment, and the tastes themselves were doubtless on different ends of the spectrum called "sweet"?

But is there, I wonder, any deeper coherence in these two amazing actions—anything that Jesus' actions are trying to say in each—or in both together? Maybe Amazing Grace sounds like this: "Drink to love, but don't try to sell it." Relationships—personal, communal, spiritual—can and must be worked on. But they can never be undertaken simply as transactions, trades, exchanges; they are always gift. And when the regularity of living (even the rigor of trying to live religiously) dulls our awareness of this utter giftedness, Amazing Grace says something else: Here! Cleanse your palates with the taste of fresh wine!

C. S. Lewis has a line that describes what has been at play at a wedding feast and in a temple courtyard: "Every idea of God we form, God must, in mercy, shatter." Stories of Amazing Grace are Tales of Holy Terror. *Every* idea of God we form, God *must*—in *mercy*—*shatter.*

Great and tender God: Set us free from all that dulls our senses to the bracing sweetness of your Amazing Grace.

Start Life Over with a Brand New Map!

Birth Pangs and Boundary Issues

JOHN 3:1–13; 4:1–41

'Twas grace that taught my heart to fear, and
    grace my fears relieved.
How precious did that grace appear the hour
    I first believed.

Amazing grace, how sweet the sound—What sort of a sound is that? Not what we expected, nothing we could have predicted—anything but the comfortable and familiar!

- ∾ "Splash! Sip! Celebration! Almost two hundred gallons of the greatest wine! Amazing!"
- ∾ "Crack! Crash! Cacophony! Disruption at the heart of the religious health care delivery system! Amazing!"

What is the sweet sound of Amazing Grace? "Drink to love, but don't try to sell it! Cleanse your palates with the taste of fresh wine!"

The writer of John's Gospel says very little about how the parties involved react when they are confronted with these intrusive "signs." But now we click open two more windows on Amazing Grace, and the parties involved do respond in ways that suggest in more detail how amazing, and precious, grace can be.

'Twas grace that taught my heart to fear, and grace my fears relieved.

- Grace relieves fear? Of course. (After all, realizing that you don't have to worry about running out of wine at the most important party of your life can reduce your anxiety level enormously.)
- Grace teaches fear? Might well be. (If a whip cutting a wide swath across the middle of your religious rituals doesn't put the fear of God in you, probably nothing will.)

But can grace do both—for the same person, at the same time? Let's invite two new recipients of Amazing Grace to have their say.

They are very different, these two.

- One is male, one female.
- The man is highly educated with significant social status. The woman presumably has no formal education, and certainly no more status than that which her society affords its women—quite possibly even less.
- He is Jewish, she a Samaritan.
- He comes at night, she at noon.
- He is respectful, even deferential. She is skeptical and makes no bones about asserting it.
- He seems, in fact, so passive as to be almost non-participative. She is insightful, quick, engaging.
- Both of them are on a spiritual journey, however, taking readings from a trusted compass of religious tradition. And both, in the presence of Jesus, find themselves disoriented.

Listen to the sound of Amazing Grace—teaching their hearts to fear—and grace their fears relieving:

Now there was a Pharisee named Nicodemus, a leader of the Jews. He came to Jesus by night and said to him, "Rabbi, we know that you are a teacher who has come from God; for no one can do these signs that you do apart from the presence of God." Jesus answered him, "Very truly, I tell you, no one can see the kingdom of God without being born from above." Nicodemus said to him, "How can anyone be born after having grown old? Can one enter a second time into the mother's womb and be born?" Jesus answered, "Very truly, I tell you, no one can enter the kingdom of God without being born of water and Spirit. What is born of the flesh is flesh, and what is born of the Spirit is spirit. Do not be astonished that I said to you, 'You must be born from above.' The wind blows where it chooses, and you hear the sound of it, but you do not know where it comes from or where it goes. So it is with everyone who is born of the Spirit." Nicodemus said to him, "How can these things be?" Jesus answered him, "Are you a teacher of Israel, and yet you do not understand these things?" (3:1–10)

It is to his credit that Nicodemus comes at all, don't you think? As a Pharisee, he is not directly involved in the workings of the temple; yet, in the wake of the tumultuous temple encounter just recounted by the Evangelist, I find it fascinating that Nicodemus begins by designating Jesus as "a teacher who has come from

God," and that, by implication, he understands the "signs" that Jesus has done not only as remarkable, but also as God-inspired.

Coming to visit Jesus takes more than mere curiosity; it requires a measure of courage and imagination. Nicodemus knows a great deal already, and he seems eager to learn more—more than willing to entertain a further extending of the orderly universe he already knows so well.

Jesus, without observing those polite introductories apart from which no social interaction can smoothly commence, throws down a theological gauntlet—lets fly with a phrase that sets his visitor's compass spinning, "I say to you for certain, Nicodemus, you must be born again."

Nicodemus politely raises a reasonable objection concerning the biological improbability of this curious injunction. And yet this man is no fool. I don't think that he's really confused about what he is hearing, do you? I think he has a more than tacit sense of where Jesus may be trying to push him.

How much time has it taken Nicodemus to amass the considerable curriculum vitae he has acquired? College, seminary, and graduate school memories, for some of us at least, become fond memories only as they become *distant* ones. Having achieved professional status the hard way—by working for it—would most of us give it all up and go back to day one of freshman orientation? Jesus is asking a lot!

Not just born again, he tells Nicodemus, but born from above as well! New theological credentialing, this time around, must come not as well-deserved achievement, but as God's gracious gift! (If I really have to return to kindergarten and work my way back up to another PhD, at least I want it said of me that I earned it—every last paper, every last course. I want no hint of favoritism or reverse age discrimination dogging my second career!)

Perhaps Nicodemus is not a "theological over-achiever." (The text certainly does not say so.) Maybe reading theology all over again would not, in his mind, be such a bad thing. But what if that entailed not just doing it again, but doing it very differently? What if the slate has to be wiped clean, and one has to begin again without any sense of clear direction?

"Sorry, Nicodemus, but that's how it is," says Jesus, with what sounds like no sympathy whatsoever. "Spiritual discernment comes to you like the wind. Knowing the tradition like you do, you of all people should be aware of that already. You know your Isaiah: 'Do not remember the former things—behold I am doing a new thing among you.' The modus operandi of Spirit-work is to blow from out of seeming nowhere, bringing new worlds to life."

"How can these things be?" protests the harried theologian. Is Nicodemus's query a genuine question concerning the mechanics of spiritual causation? Is it a protest? A stall? Or might it just be the frantic, involuntary, visceral flail of a man hopelessly swept into sheer vertigo? This is not armchair theological speculation—this is scary stuff.

This conversation begins with Nicodemus saying, "We know . . ." It ends with Jesus hanging a haunting question: "Are you a teacher, and yet you don't know these things?" Which way is True North? The compass doesn't seem to say. An elder, a male, begins to feel something of new life spasms that, under most circumstances, only overtake you if you are young and female. I have a sneaking suspicion, don't you, that Grace is teaching this man to fear!

∽℮

[Jesus] came to a Samaritan city called Sychar, near the plot of ground that Jacob had given to his son Joseph. Jacob's well was there, and Jesus, tired out by his journey, was sitting by the well. It was about noon. A Samaritan woman came to draw water, and Jesus said to her, "Give me a drink." (His disciples had gone to the city to buy food.) The Samaritan woman said to him, "How is it that you, a Jew, ask a drink of me, a woman of Samaria?" (4:5–9)

In the world of my religious upbringing, to begin the reading of this familiar story was instantly to invoke a whole set of interpretive moral and soteriological assumptions: She's a woman, a Samaritan, and a bad one— living, as she is, with a non-husband after having gone through five. And very tired, but good, kind Jesus sees her for the sinner that she is, forgives her anyway, and offers her the precious gift of Living Water. At first she changes the subject; but Jesus persists, eventually she repents, accepts his gift, and runs to tell her friends— and they all live happily ever after—Amazing Grace!

From my present vantage point, however, I am not at all sure that sinfulness, repentance, or forgiveness are central to this Amazing Grace encounter.

No transcripts from seminary in her file, no standing in her community as a scholar or spiritual leader, the woman from Samaria who comes to the well turns out (in the light of the noonday sun) to be much less in the dark than Nicodemus. She is a street-smart theologian and a far more spirited dialogue partner for Jesus than the one described as "a ruler of the Jews." Far more challenging, venturesome, imaginative—maybe even more aware of how much is hanging upon a discussion that (unlike Nicodemus) she does not initiate.

"Our ancestors worshipped on this mountain, but you say that the place where people must worship is Jerusalem" (4:20).

"That"—so ran the standard Amazing Grace sermon from the church of my childhood—"was a dodge. She didn't want to face the truth about her wretched moral condition (five husbands plus—harrumpf!). When Jesus got too close to where she really was, like all of us sinners, she tried desperately to distract him from the issue at hand."

Frankly, I think the question of where one stands for worship *is* the issue. Placeless worship tends to be empty worship, worship in the abstract. Prayers addressed "to Whom it may concern" are often addressed to no one in particular. A God "who is everywhere," however tolerant and enlightened that might sound, often comes down, in terms of practical prayer, to be a God of nowhere.

"I'm very spiritual, just not very religious. I believe in God, I just can't abide denominations and institutions." Such sentiments are currently common currency. They are not often accompanied by discipline and sacrificial commitment. Of course it makes a difference upon which mountain one takes a stand to worship!

Religious turf wars and ensuing cycles of bloodshed and violence notwithstanding, at least there is this to be said for the woman's claim: where you stand or kneel when you worship is important. Connected with the earth, with particularities of time, place, community, ritual, sacred text, and tradition, one has a far better chance of making connection with that which transcends them all. This woman is no more a fool than Nicodemus is. She has a point—and it goes to the heart of what incarnational theology is all about— both God's revelation and human response only come to particular persons in particular places, to particular communities in particular ways. The live encounter of incarnation may be available to everyone, everywhere; but the fact remains: there is no such thing as a "generic incarnation."

Jesus, however, takes the assumptions implicit in her assertive theological question and turns them inside out. He snatches the two-dimensional religious map toward which she is orienting (where X marks the spot) and plunges her, head over heels, into her own experience of spiritual vertigo: "The hour is coming, and is now here, when the true worshipers will worship the Father in spirit and truth, for the Father seeks such as these to worship him. God is spirit, and those who worship him must worship in spirit and truth" (4:23–24).

Spirit and truth? Where, for God's sake, is that? What kind of spiritual geography is this? It's totally disorienting, downright cruel! Jesus could have told her: "Woman, you are religiously turned around. You are going west. You need to head east. Go back five hundred miles, take the left fork in the road, and you will end up right where you need to be." Had he done that, the woman could have responded either: "Thanks ever so much for your help," or "I'm going to stick with the map I've got."

As it is, however, the whole notion of religious boundaries and directions has been stood upon its head. Not that there aren't any. But they can't be mapped out on flat surfaces. Because Amazing Grace is, simultaneously, a pulsing center point *and* an all-surrounding, boundary-bursting sphere. Therefore, the task of finding religious boundary markers and establishing one's spiritual bearings takes on an entirely new dimension.

Do you hear what I hear? In the words of Jesus, Amazing Grace is teaching this woman's heart to fear as well. (And, in the end, different from Nicodemus as she can be, she meets up with him at that Holy Terror place where your heart freezes and everything that's in your head begins to spin.)

Grace has taught their hearts to fear, then. The question, however, is: Does grace their fears relieve? (And if so, does it do so with any substance—in some way other than a simple sheepish assertion: "Scared you, huh? Well, not to worry, everything will turn out all right in the end.")

∾

Storyteller John gives us two quick, suggestive, down-the-road glances at Nicodemus. The man himself makes only cameo appearances, but the Evangelist sets up both scenes elaborately and with high drama.

Scene One: Jesus has fed the five thousand, and after an extended discussion, driven off crowds of would-be simple faith believers ("Just give us bread, and we'll follow you anywhere; ask us to eat your flesh, however, and we're out of here"). He returns from this discussion to face his brothers, who urge him to attend the Festival of Booths and put on a spiritual fireworks display (because, in fact, they don't deeply believe in him any more than the loaf and fish eaters do).

On his own timetable (like the one he pulled out in Cana), Jesus eventually does show up at the festival— and takes on the hostile cross-examination of still more skeptics. Opinions about him, hot and heavy, are divided. The police are called in. Jesus keeps talking. Bewildered, the police return empty-handed. An ugly scene unfolds, as religious know-it-alls snarl down their noses at a crowd that "does not know the law," and is "accursed."

A hand is raised; a voice is cleared in this debate amongst the ruling religious intelligentsia. Both hand and voice belong to Nicodemus. "Our law does not judge people without first giving them a hearing to find out what they are doing, does it?" (7:51).

In a heartbeat, the scorn turns vitriolic—on Nicodemus. "Surely you are not also from Galilee, are you? Search and you will see that no prophet is to arise from Galilee" (7:52). (They have a map, these knowledgeable spiritual geographers, and the X on Galilee is conspicuous by its absence.)

What does Nicodemus have to gain by raising his perfectly justified objection? It is by no means out of line with the tradition that has nurtured him, and that he honors. But his colleagues seem to have lost sight of that. Politically, Nicodemus has a lot to lose! And what if Jesus is, in fact, an oh-so-clever blasphemer, a counterfeiter of tradition, rather than a radical adherent?

But perhaps it is his birthing new life that Nicodemus is concerned about, not his world of influence. *How precious does that grace appear, the hour he first believes!* That line ought not to be inappropriately accessed as a simplistic bumper sticker. Yet (especially in light of his subsequent experience—redescribed below), I can make a case for saying that Nicodemus is manifesting a whole new understanding of the Spirit that blows—where it will, surely—but as the ever-renewing energy that gives life to "the letter of the Law." Perhaps the "signs" to which he made initial reference are now more than matters of curiosity, and have become a means of connection with the one whom he had earlier so tenuously sought out.

Scene Two: Jesus is dead. Crucified, but still hanging. To identify with one who has been executed owing to the strange collusion of religious and political interests, especially when there's nothing left to be done for him—this is tantamount to political, maybe physical, suicide. But up steps Nicodemus. John takes care to make sure we remember that Nicodemus "had at first come to Jesus by night" (19:39). Here he comes, in broad daylight (as he comes to the argument with his colleagues), now bowed under the weight of one hundred pounds of spices. He is not inconspicuous. Together, with Joseph of Arimathea, he takes the corpse of Jesus and "wrap[s] it with the spices in linen cloths, according to the burial custom of the Jews" (19:40). Then he lays the body in a tomb.

Why? What sense does this make? None, unless he has awakened to the fact that he is being born from above into a quality of Life Eternal that utterly neutralizes the power of any death threat either Rome or Jerusalem can brandish. So precious does that grace appear, he is willing to risk his life for it. Grace, I think, has this man's "fear relieved." Not eradicated, necessarily, but framed in a context that enables him, regardless of the consequences, to answer a higher calling with courage.

~e

What of the woman from Samaria? Storyteller John doesn't keep us in suspense about her. Jesus, having addressed her very reasonable map-reading question with a disorienting, boundary-bursting word, now reorients her to the Very Word, the Living Water that he is (water that can, in fact, erupt as a spring from any given mountain).

Does she really understand what she is hearing, this highly inquisitive, resourceful woman? Maybe so, maybe not. "He cannot be the Messiah, can he?" she asks, sharing with others the effervescence within her that may still be impossible for her to fathom. (How often do we say, in the face of what fulfils our deepest longings, highest hopes: "That's just too good to be true!") Be that as it may, she certainly seems to be saying by her actions what Nicodemus has said with his: *How precious did that grace appear, the hour I first believed.* So precious, in fact, that it is far too valuable to keep—just as it is impossible to hoard.

Whatever her misgivings, they do not keep this

woman from bearing witness to what she has encountered. Head still spinning, I am guessing, she manages to find her way back to the city, and, by the energy of her continuing theological questions, she draws her whole community into a celebration not entirely unlike the wedding feast at Cana.

John, the teller of this disquieting tale, doesn't say so in as many words, but I'll tell you what I think: Grace has this woman's "fears relieved" as well. Whatever apprehensions she still may have, whatever constrictions her social situation may impose, they do not squelch her singing in the slightest.

◦◦

Two long, grace-filled conversations. Two grace-redirected lifelong journeys. Mark it well: A total reorientation of our sense of God's True North almost never happens overnight. A clear, complete sense of spiritual direction seldom, if ever, deeply develops in an instant flash. Grace is amazing, all right, but it is not necessarily sudden. You wake up seventeen years later and quietly say: Oh, yeah! Why, yes! Of course! Makes sense! In some ways I've known this all along. What grace!

But the fact remains, grace breaks in when every idea of God we've formed, God has, in mercy, shattered. If you aren't sure that this is so, go have a talk with

Nicodemus and the woman from Samaria. With both of them, Jesus brings on birth pangs and broaches boundary issues. The sweet sound of Amazing Grace sometimes says shocking things like, "Start life over with a brand-new map!"

Great and tender God: Disorient our lives with Holy Fear, that we may perceive—again, and from above—the precious appearing of your Amazing Grace.

Don't Throw Rocks Without Good Eyes!

*Misdirected Accusations and
Directed Acquittals*

JOHN 8:1–11; 9:1–41

The Lord has promised good to me, his word
   my hope secures.
He will my shield and portion be as long as
   life endures.

What is the sweet sound of Amazing Grace? That is the question we are posing to various folks in John's Gospel, all of whom have grace encounters that leave them shaking their heads, gasping for breath.

What did grace sound like when you heard it? How, exactly, was grace sweet? Sugar sweet? Sharp sweet? Bittersweet? Not just grace, the abstract idea; grace, the pious platitude; grace, the sentimental gush—but grace as you actually encountered it.

There is no "one size fits all" generic sound of grace, we are beginning to suspect. So we are asking, from one recipient after another, how did the shattering sound of Amazing Grace break upon *you*?

The answers to our question have begun to pour in.

"Grace," say a bride and groom, wedding guests, and servants, "is like gallons and gallons of wedding wine coming out of nowhere."

"Grace," say those on all sides of temple court transactions, "is like having your tables overturned by a whirling whip."

"Grace," says Nicodemus, "is like starting God-school all over again when you thought you had a PhD."

"Grace," says a woman from Samaria, "is like finding God, not here or there, but in every conceivable place at once—where nobody can say (as I first assumed), 'This is our territory—trespassers will be prosecuted!'"

"Grace," say they all, "is like sheer vertigo—getting turned inside out and upside down—Amazing!"

Now we put the question to a woman caught in adultery, a man born blind, and a group of folks who take their social, moral, and religious responsibilities very seriously: "Tell us, what does grace look, sound, smell, taste, feel like to each of you?" We know that whatever they tell us, we won't know just how any of them feels (nobody ever knows just how anybody else feels). But if we pay attention, we might just find a common point of meeting, a useful reference point from which to share our insights and deepen our own understandings.

So, to set the stage, let's ask another question first: What does it feel like to be judged?

- ~ Maybe judged literally—in a courtroom; probably not for murder, but maybe for a minor traffic violation. A black-robed judge, sitting behind a large, high desk. Not smiling.
- ~ Maybe judged in a contest, if not for your Olympic skating prowess, perhaps for your speaking, your singing, or your blueberry pie. Blue ribbon? Red ribbon? No, "Honorable Mention." (Everyone gets "Honorable Mention.")
- ~ Maybe you have been judged, not literally, but just as truly—with a cutting word, a withering look. In any case, judged, sealed into a box with a preprinted label pasted on top.

From deep inside, feelings of frustration well up when we are judged: "That's not fair!" We want to protest, to defend ourselves, to justify our positions. But sooner or later we usually give up on such attempts because they are systematically ignored, summarily refuted, or turned around and used as further evidence against us.

So I have some sympathy for the woman caught in adultery and for the man born blind, don't you—surrounded as both of them are, by judges? I don't know just how either of them feels. But I feel a certain compassion for them both.

The woman. She's been caught in adultery ("in the very act," her accusers tell Jesus). But, of course, she has had some help. (The last time I checked with a moral theologian, I was informed that one cannot commit adultery alone.) Furthermore, especially in light of the social dynamics in play at the time, it isn't clear that she was the one who chose to initiate the interaction. "Blame the victim" is not a game invented yesterday.

The man born blind is a victim of a different sort. His blindness, as such, can be dealt with—as it often is by those who are blind, with a resourcefulness that outstrips that of the ordinarily sighted.

What he cannot control, this man blind from birth, is what others make of his blindness. This man is not just judged; he is judged four times over, from four different angles.

"Sticks and stones will break my bones, but words will never hurt," you used to shout back on the grade school playground when verbal bullies were having their way at your expense. You said it precisely because it wasn't true. Words do hurt. Words can kill. Verbal stones crush.

Listen to the stones as they come crashing in on the poor blind man:

- "He's a sinner," say the disciples (or at the very least, he has inherited the infection of those who have brought him into being).
- "He's not someone we can clearly identify," is the consensus of his neighbors. (Apart from his handicap, they cannot be sure they even recognize him.)
- "He's a Sabbath subverter," charge the religious legal minds. (He can't help the fact he was at the wrong place at the wrong time when this healing energy was released. But the man is responsible, nonetheless—as responsible as he was, in the eyes of Jesus' disciples, for his condition initially.)
- And the man's own parents—"How was he healed? He's an adult. We can't speak for him. He can speak up for himself." (This is the judgment that really cuts, being so close to home. In fear for their vulnerable position, the man's parents treat him as though he were a stranger.)

The man is not in double jeopardy; he is in quadruple jeopardy: "The verdict is in. Don't waste our time trying to file an appeal."

But—our sympathy for the man born blind has blinded us, has it not? It has led us in the direction of judging his judges—not altogether unlike some of the ways in which they have judged him! They have reasons, all of them, these judges, for the verdicts they have rendered—viable reasons, in every case.

- ◌ The disciples are just trying to make sense of human tragedy in theological terms by employing a standard explanation that has been used the world over from time immemorial—an explanation taught them by their parents, who learned it from their parents, who got it from—guess where? The story of Job would have counted for something against such an explanation in their minds, surely; but even Jesus in their very presence (as reported in other Gospels) seemed to associate healing and forgiveness (and, by implication, suffering and sin).
- ◌ The neighbors have their own lives to live, which doesn't leave them the leisure to attend in close detail to everyone whose paths they cross. Recognition is primarily contextual—have you never walked right past someone who is familiar to you in one

place but, in a different context, barely touches your awareness?

~ The parents—they are justifiably terrified. It's not just that their status is in jeopardy as members of the synagogue. Loss of participation there (unlike what excommunication would entail in a secular society like ours) would bring ostracism from every aspect of social life. Without denying their son, they would be as good as dead.

~ And the Pharisees. Easy, it is, to demonize them, but they are only defending the fabric that sustains an entire way of life. Not unlike judges who have to make difficult calls in individual cases that result indirectly in personal hardship.

The bottom line is, in making difficult judgments, we all do what we think is right. And what damage such judgments can do before we come, in retrospect, to realize how wrong we were!

Epidemic, isn't it? Misjudgments that trash careers. Suspicions that sabotage relationships. Planes that slam into towers. Bombs that rain down upon children. Children that, as suicide bombers, obliterate other children. Judges, everywhere judges!

Well, thank God Jesus is around. He won't judge the woman caught in adultery. He won't judge the judges of the blind—Amazing Grace!

Hold on. Wait a minute. Not so fast. Jesus *is* judging, in fact.

- ∾ What does he say to the stone-holding judges who surround the convicted woman? "Let him without sin cast the first stone" (8:7). Just do it.
- ∾ What does he say to the judges of the man born blind? "I came into this world for judgment so that those who do not see may see, and those who do see may become blind" (9:39).

Well, there it is. At the end of the day—all of us judges are judged.

But it makes a difference what we mean by the word *judgment*. Robert Farrar Capon, in a splendid little book called *The Youngest Day: Shelter Island's Seasons in the Light of Grace,* compares the four last things: Death, Judgment, Hell, and Heaven, to the four seasons: winter, spring, summer, and autumn.

- ∾ Death, he says, is winter. (That seems obvious enough.)

- Hell, he declares, is summer. (Makes perfect sense!)
- Heaven, he claims, is autumn (which connection, when it sinks in, is lovely).
- That leaves Judgment to be seen with spring (which doesn't seem to fit at all).

"This just shows," Capon replies to our disbelieving protest, "how little we understand of judgment—at least as God undertakes it."

Judgment, Capon continues, is *not* the same as condemnation. Indeed, condemnation is the antithesis of judgment. Judgment, asserts Capon, has to do with clear and wise discernment. Spring, he concludes, is the season in the gentle light of which we are able to discern, after a long dark winter, between that which is truly dead and that which has been merely awaiting the opportunity to spring forth into new life. Spring is the season in which it is possible to discern what kind of leaf, flower, and fruit will come forth from *this* plant, and from *that*.

"God sent not his son into the world to condemn the world," says Jesus to Nicodemus (or as John the storyteller, via King James's translators, observes in reflecting on their encounter). "God sent not his son into the world to condemn the world, but that the world through him might be saved" (3:17).

So what, then, are we to make of "Let him who is without sin cast the first stone"?

Preacher Gene Lowry, attending to the story text with soft-focused eyes (rather than beady ones) shows us this—a line in the story that practically nobody notices: "When they heard it, they went away, one by one, beginning with the elders" (8:9).

When permission comes from Jesus to commence with the hail of stones, says Lowry, all turn toward the oldest man. By virtue of his age, this old man evidences, *prima facie,* in the eyes of those in his day, the blessing of God for a righteous life.

But this one old man, in the light of Jesus' haunting, judging, discerning question, sees, perhaps for the first time, the truth about himself. "I'm a sinner. I can't throw the stone. I'm out of here," he says—and walks away.

Eyes now turn to the next oldest man. But how can he presume to throw a stone, when someone older (and presumably more righteous) has already left the scene? Impossible. Home goes Elder Number Two. The rest, as they say, is history. It's a scene of condemning dominoes going down, one after the other.

The judges leave because they have learned, with Jesus' provocative but spacious words, to become *judges.* Imagine what might be released in a community if even a few therein could hear the word of Amazing Grace: "Neither do I condemn you. Go your way, and . . . sin no more" (8:11). (And, one might add, "Do what you can, with the forgiving freedom you have been granted, to reweave the fabric of relationships that have been torn apart by the act you have committed.")

If I can come to see myself as deeply known but not condemned, I will have little impetus for, or interest in, pointing fingers or throwing rocks. The inexorable cycle of judgment producing destruction, and destruction bringing down judgment, has, at last, some chance of being graciously interdicted.

Jesus has, I think, a discerning, saving word for would-be rock throwers the world over. Parrying misdirected accusations with directed verdicts, that word of grace is simply this: "Only throw rocks if you've got good eyes." Healing power surges forth when, by forgiveness, condemning judgment is transformed into discerning judgment.

What is the sweet sound of Amazing Grace ringing in our ears? I think it goes like this:

> The Lord has promised good to me, his word
> my hope secures.
> He will my shield and portion be as long as
> life endures.

~ *My shield*—my sure defense against condemning judgments, whoever hurls them. Both the

woman taken in adultery and the man born
blind can surely testify to the truth of that.
Such grace, for them, must seem amazing.

ᴄ *My portion*—my never-failing resource of in-
sight, born of recognizing myself as forgiven,
thereby freed for making careful, wise, discerning judgments of my own.

Neither the man born blind nor the woman taken in
adultery are simply shielded or provided for, however.
The words of healing and forgiveness they receive are
not magical amulets—time-release capsules that pro-
vide instant fixes for all the difficulties and challenges
their respective situations have entailed or will con-
tinue to create.

What is rendered "secure" is not their situation
but their "hope"—a hope based not on what has been
provided for them in that moment, but on what that
provision symbolizes in the "promised good" they can
henceforth count on "as long as life endures." What
is that unfailing promise? Continuing Amazing Grace
adjudication at the hand of the One whose judgments
alone are always just and true.

God's grace is always God's promised good judgment; God's word our hope secures. God's judgment is
always God's Amazing Grace. Not what we would expect. Not that with which we are either comfortable or

familiar. But then, the truth of the matter is this: Every idea of God we form—God must, in mercy, shatter.

≈

Great and tender God: Grant us the grace to recognize and receive your good judgment. And the good judgment to recognize and receive your Amazing Grace.

4

Cut Through the Tomb Tapes, Let Down Your Hair!

Certain Death and Eternal Life

JOHN 11:1-44; 12:1-9

Through many dangers, toils, and snares
    I have already come.
'Tis grace has brought me safe thus far, and
    grace will lead me home.

We are on an unfolding adventure into the deep mystery of Amazing Grace. You have come, by now, to expect a back and forth, a push and pull between two striking phrases:

- One from John Newton—"Amazing grace! How sweet the sound." (Newton's own testimony of transformation from wretched slave trader to forgiven freedom singer)

∽ One from C. S. Lewis—"Every idea of God we form, God must, in mercy, shatter." (Lewis's one-line summary of a life "surprised by joy")

How can both of these phrases be true simultaneously?

∽ Amazing Grace—God our safety.
∽ Shattering mercy—God the threat.

The first can make God sound sweet as sugar candy. But the second sounds like the disconcerting claim that God is the Cosmic Bull in the human china shop! Life is fragile enough as it is without such a God around to make things worse. Is there nothing about God we can trust? With the help of yet another story from John's Gospel, let's try to close in on this hanging question.

The first thing to say, before we even start to hear the story of Mary and Jesus at Bethany is this: the interplay between safety and threat is absolutely essential to every adventure that is worth the time and trouble of the trip. Safety and threat—mixed up together—are right at the heart of every story we have ever heard that was at all worth telling. What are the marks of a high adventure, a good story? What are we listening for when somebody commences with that familiar phrase "once upon a time"?

We are listening, in a story, for interesting characters—folks who are not "just like us," but with whom we have some point of contact. We are on the listen for those with whom we can identify, and for those who serve as stand-ins of a sort for other people, good and bad, that we already know or are concerned about. We are listening, as well, for scenes, settings, and circumstances that hold some fascination for us—places and conditions that, from a safe distance, we would like to explore.

More than that, we are listening for action—for conflict, threat, suspense, drama. Character and setting are necessary, but they are not sufficient. We want a plot—a plot that thickens. ("Once upon a time there were some nice people, and they lived a nice life." That does not rank high on the list of good short stories.)

Last, we lean in, not just with our ears but with our bodies, awaiting a satisfying resolution to the story. Let's call this the "happily ever after" element in storytelling.

Don't dismiss that last criterion with a shrug. There is a legitimate place in stories for "happily ever after." If you are reading a bedtime story to a young child, you want one that ends this way—unless you want to be up for the rest of the night. And, truth be told, the child in most of us wants an appropriate adult equivalent when we reach for a novel or a TV remote control at the end of a long, hard day.

But there is a downside, is there not, to stories that keep ending with everyone living "happily ever after"—because that is seldom the way things unfold in real life. (Has your life been just one "happily ever after," following hard upon another?)

Human tragedies arise when our ideals of "happily ever after" come crashing down, or come into collision course with the ideals of others. (Jerusalem, for example, is an embodied symbol of "happily ever after" for Israelis and Palestinians alike. "Happily ever after" for followers of George W. Bush does not peacefully co-exist with "happily ever after" for followers of Osama bin Laden or Saddam Hussein.) Indeed, one of the most persistent sources of shattered human hopes and dreams is the employment of utopian visions of "happily ever after" as inspiration and justification to impose "our" story on "their" story.

Our deepest feelings of wound and outrage arise when we sense that "things should not have turned out this way." Hence our ambivalence; we want happy endings, but don't much trust them. And we don't much trust those who do trust in them. They are, as we say, "too good to be true." Regardless of what C. S. Lewis may say, a shattered life never feels like a mercy.

But brokenness and wholeness, conflict and resolution, are not always as easy to distinguish definitively as they might seem to be. In our efforts, for ourselves or for each other, to "make things all better," curing is not necessarily the same as healing.

I have a friend who used to be a radiation oncologist. He had a corner office with a window that enabled him to observe his patients as they made their way into the Medical Arts complex for their appointments with him. Often, he told me, there would be on the desk in front of him the medical record of an incoming patient indicating a clean bill of physical health. The approaching face of the person corresponding to the name on the record, however, would sometimes look like death warmed over. On the other hand, the faces of patients whose records clearly indicated that their medical conditions were terminal, he said, often radiated an aura of deep spiritual health. Many are cured who are not healed; many are healed who are not cured. What it means to live "happily ever after" is not always obvious.

Once upon a time . . . So begins today's story of Amazing Grace from John's Gospel.

> A certain man was ill, Lazarus of Bethany, the
> village of Mary and her sister Martha. Mary was
> the one who anointed the Lord with perfume
> and wiped his feet with her hair; her brother
> Lazarus was ill. So the sisters sent a message to
> Jesus, "Lord, he whom you love is ill." (11:1–3)

I don't need to quote you any more, do I? You probably know exactly how the story goes, from one scene to the next, and how it turns out in the end. You know the story by title: "The Raising of Lazarus." At first hearing the Lazarus story sounds like a perfectly straightforward narrative instance ending predictably in "happily ever after." But the longer and closer we listen, the stranger the story becomes. And before long, it doesn't sound much like "happily ever after" at all. Consider:

- There is an opening, situation-setting, and character-designating sentence. ("A certain man was ill, Lazarus of Bethany, the village of Mary and her sister Martha.") So far, so good—that's what stories are supposed to do.
- But now listen to the next sentence: "Mary was the one who anointed the Lord with perfume and wiped his feet with her hair."

Maybe this notation has been inserted to remind us of something we have already heard about this character named Mary so that it will be fresh in our minds— at the ready for making a strategic connection with a scene or action soon to follow. (That is a frequently employed technique in storytelling art.) So let's go back a few pages in the story text to find the scene to which the Gospel author is making reference.

- Back we go, from chapter ten, through nine, eight, and seven. No reference to the character, scene, or action in question.
- Well, let's start from the beginning—no such activity described in chapters one through three.
- Was it in the middle? A check of chapters four to six reveals no reference to the event.

Where is it, then? We know it has to be in the story somewhere!

And then, paging ahead, we find the scene that chapter eleven alludes to—in chapter twelve! Is this odd, or what? John the Evangelist has stolen his own thunder—gotten ahead of himself, introduced a later scene before depicting the current one! Either we need to send this author back to Story Writing 101, or something very strange is going on. This is not the way stories are supposed to go! A problem, surely; but let it pass for the moment, and look at the other features of the story.

- Lazarus is sick. Jesus delays in coming— deliberately. (Okay, that's well within the bounds of good storytelling technique. It heightens the suspense.) Yet such delay seems decidedly out of character for one who in other places is dubbed not "the dithering doctor" but "the Great Physician."

꙳ The storyteller does have Jesus say something to the effect that "this is for God's glory." But, frankly, this sounds very much as though Jesus is jerking Mary and Martha around for the sake of divine theological theatrics (not all that different from what Jesus seems to suggest about the "reason" for the condition of the man born blind). Everybody, so it seems, is being used to make a point. Good storytellers don't moralize like this, nor do they let their characters do their preaching.

꙳ Notice, next, that when he gets to the tomb, Jesus weeps. Not once or twice or even three times does the story bring this to our attention. We hear it four times over, in one form or another. And this means that when we get to the triumphant punch line: "Lazarus, come out!" it is altogether likely that the stains of Jesus' tears are still deeply etched in the sweat of his face. It means that rather than calling forth Lazarus à la Cecil B. DeMille, when Jesus raises Lazarus, the supposedly sweet sound of Amazing Grace is a wrenching cry of utter anguish.

What is this storyteller thinking? What could he be wanting us to think? But now (to make what is already very curious more perplexing still) do you notice what the story *doesn't* say? There is no word whatsoever from Lazarus. Nor even a word from the omniscient narrator about what Lazarus said or did or felt.

The natural inclination might be to think that Lazarus, being brought back to life, would be happy as a clam. That may, however, be simplistic. In Rock Creek Cemetery near Washington D.C., there is a life-sized sculpture of Lazarus just emerging from the tomb. No delight or excitement lights up his face, nor any jaunty "I beat the odds, I'm baaack!" The face of Lazarus, instead, is a mixture of dazed disorientation and stark terror.

Is it possible, in light of all these apparent narrative oddities, that John the storyteller is signaling us, subtly but clearly, that unless there is more to resurrection than "coming back to life," it isn't worth what it takes for anyone concerned? Just because you're cured, it doesn't mean you're healed. Just because you are breathing, it doesn't mean you are living. Whatever the story of Lazarus is, in and of itself, it is not a "happily ever after."

But now, let's go back to the misplaced Mary piece of the Lazarus story—look at that, and look ahead as well to the story of which she is the central focus. It is almost as if the Evangelist is so intent on telling us Mary's story that he just can't keep from interrupting himself as he tells the story of Lazarus. Or maybe John is taking awkward literary pains to ensure that we see very clearly: this is *not* your normal "happily ever after."

Here is how John at last begins his description of what he has previously and cryptically alluded to:

> Six days before the Passover Jesus came to Bethany, the home of Lazarus, whom he had raised from the dead. There they gave a dinner for him. Martha served, and Lazarus was one of those at the table with him. Mary took a pound of costly perfume made of pure nard, anointed Jesus' feet, and wiped them with her hair. The house was filled with the fragrance of the perfume. (12:1–3)

This should be a happy meal. Prominently present is Lazarus, recently brought back to life. Should not everyone be celebrating with abandon? But no—death is in the air—so thick, in fact, the certainty of its looming immanence is all but suffocating. What, after all, do you say at supper to Jesus, who, having raised Lazarus, is now a dead man walking?

In comes Mary, who begins behaving very oddly

in the setting of a supper. She anoints Jesus' feet with high-end perfume and wipes them dry with the tresses of her hair. Can you savor the sweet sound and scent of Amazing Grace in what her actions sing?

> Through many dangers, toils, and snares
> I have already come.
> 'Tis grace that brought me safe thus far,
> and grace will lead me home.

Mary is not looking to deny or to escape the threat of death. Surrounded by the very stench of death, she is celebrating with abandon the fresh aroma of eternal life.

"Unbind him, and let him go!" Jesus summarily commanded the mourners (surely startled when they saw Lazarus emerging, still death-taped, from his tomb). Mary, I think, has taken Jesus' command to heart—and brilliantly, boldly translated it from that setting into the wider, deeper context of resurrection meaning that Jesus (with help from Holy Ghost writer John) was probably getting at to begin with.

Anointing Jesus in decisive, even defiant repudiation of the approaching horror of crucifixion, Mary has cut through all the surrounding tomb tapes and let down her hair. She is, by now, on the other side of her remarkable experience with her brother Lazarus, thoroughly realistic about "dangers, toils, and snares."

I think she senses as well that "grace" is not a product to be bagged and held on to for dear life, but rather a guiding light on a dark path, a light that "will lead [her] home"—a Person who persists as dependable Presence through an unpredictable process.

It is interesting to compare her response to Jesus here with Peter's response to Jesus one chapter later. "No, Lord, you will never wash my feet!" Peter protests, aghast, when his Lord does, at the farewell meal with his disciples, what is strikingly analogous to that which Mary does at the family farewell meal in Bethany. Jesus leaves the table at which he is the host, lays aside his dignity with his garments, and offers to his disciples what Mary has offered him—gentle, intimate touch—tangible assurance of continuing deep connection in the very face of the threatening disconnect that death both symbolizes and effects.

"No! Never!" says Peter when Jesus kneels before him—to which Jesus replies, simply but tellingly, "If you refuse this, you and I have nothing in common." Openness, vulnerability, connection—these seem such ineffective antidotes to "dangers, toils, and snares"! But they are means of grace by which we are led home. Mary, I suggest, has come to realize through the death of Lazarus what Peter will not begin to fathom until he emerges on the other side of Jesus' death and meets him again at another meal. (But that is a story for the chapter yet to come.)

One more observation, however, about the interchange that Mary initiates and that Jesus explicitly accepts (defending her vigorously against Judas who, hypocritically, challenges her spending priorities): Amazing Grace, it seems, can operate both ways.

Up to this point in John's account of the Jesus story, Jesus has been the one who offers the shattering, sweet-sounding gift to those in widely varying circumstances of need. But here, now, she offers grace to him. And he is not too proud to receive for himself what he offers to others. (There is not a hint from him of "Thank you very much, but I cannot accept what you are offering— *I'm* the one who gives Amazing Grace!")

Sacred connection (as opposed to religious transaction) has mutuality about it, not just contractual reciprocities. Mary has learned, as a grateful recipient of grace, that she can offer grace as well. And who knows but whether that gift, gratefully accepted by Jesus, does not become a source of spiritual energy for him as he offers grace to his gathered disciples one last time before his Crucifixion in behavior that is as unfamiliar, uncomfortable, and convention-shattering as hers. Not simply shattering standard master-disciple conventions, but (as evidenced in his ensuing, extended, very elevated "Last Discourse") decisively redirecting the way in which we are to understand our relationship to God and to each other.

How can Mary manage, in the anguish-charged, confusing circumstances of this family meal in Bethany, to sing Amazing Grace the way she does? Because, I think, she has heard Jesus utter words that have shattered her wildest expectations:

I am resurrection.

I am life.

Come out, LAZARUS!

Come on, folks—Cut him loose and set him free!

Does Mary fully understand what she hears in that? I seriously doubt it! Not any more than the woman from Samaria or Nicodemus or anybody else we have been hearing from. Does Mary have it all figured out? Not likely! But I'll tell you what: From now on, she will do everything within her power to follow that voice to hell and back.

Why? Because this is a voice she can totally trust. Every idea she's had of God, God has, in mercy, shattered. Amazing Grace!

Great and tender God: In your good time, in your own way, speak your clear word into our tombs, and raise us in your grace.

5

Touching Is Fine, Just Don't Cling!

Hilarious Journeys and
Healing Recognitions

JOHN 20–21

When we've been there ten thousand years,
   bright shining as the sun,
We've no less days to sing God's praise than
   when we'd first begun.

I am an Episcopalian. We Episcopalians are proper
people. We do certain things in certain ways at certain
times—and *only* at certain times. Indeed, the Scripture
lessons we read—each specifically designated for particular Sundays, along with opening prayer prescribed—
are called "the propers of the day." Proper Episcopalians
do not sing Christmas carols during Advent. During
Lent we never say that four-syllable celebratory word
that begins and ends with the letter *A*—that would
be most improper. This final Amazing Grace meditation

(in embryonic form) was first presented on a Penitential Friday immediately preceding Holy Week. I stood before the congregation in fear and trembling, knowing that the good Episcopalians there would raise their eyebrows (at least) when they heard the stories from John's Gospel they were about to hear (and which we will now as well). Easter stories? In the heart of Lent? Harrumpf! Liturgical police on patrol can be quite intimidating.

You are welcome to your own "Harrumpf!" as well. But I intend to press ahead anyway, hoping it will be easier to obtain your forgiveness than your permission. For even if you are not a "proper Episcopalian," the notion of Easter stories as hilarious may strike you as, well, of questionable propriety at least!

More seriously, though (removing tongue from cheek), we simply must conclude with the Easter accounts from John's Gospel, because every other story of Amazing Grace that ever has or will be told is one that tastes and smells and sounds like Easter. That should come as no surprise, for Easter is, after all, the quintessential expression of God's Amazing Grace.

An interesting point of entry into the Amazing Grace of Easter is offered by the last verse of the hymn. You remember the words:

> When we've been there ten thousand years,
>   bright shining as the sun,

> We've no less days to sing God's praise than
>   when we'd first begun.

That's lovely to sing, but difficult to believe, and for good reason. For one thing, none of us here have yet "been there"—to that "home" where grace will one day safely lead us. We've not been there for a single hour, to say nothing of ten thousand years. How, then, could we really know that much of what it is we're singing?

But there is another reason it is hard for us to believe that "we've no less days to sing God's praise than when we'd first begun." That is because all our present experience tells us that it simply isn't so.

- "Time's up! Turn in your test papers!"
- "Time to come in now—playtime is over!"
  "Please, can't we stay out a little longer?"
  "No! We're already late; we don't have time."
- "I'm sorry, but I just don't have any time for you right now."
- "It was time for him to go." (My friend was talking not about the termination of his father's job, but the termination of his father's life.)

Time may march on, as far as our clocks are concerned, but for living creatures, time is forever coming to an end. "To everything there is a time and season—a time to be born, and a time to die." The one business that never goes out of business, is the business of burying those for whom Time is up.

To know that, however, doesn't make it any easier to cope with. Indeed, lots of folks invest lots of energy in the denial of death—usually with disastrous results for all concerned. We sometimes try to cope with Time's Up by avoiding the end as long as possible: "Please, doctor, isn't there anything you can do to give us just a little more time with Grandma?" But sooner or later, we have to come to terms with the inevitable.

Which is exactly what three people in John's Gospel are trying to do as they begin to cope with Jesus' death. Their names are Mary Magdalene, Thomas, and Peter. All three are doing their best to deal with the cruel fate they have been dealt. Each, in his or her own way, is trying, as we say, to get closure on a life that, once upon a time, had a name called Jesus. All of them are getting on with the grief process, but they are having a hard time dealing with Time's Up for Jesus—because it feels for all the world like Time's Up for them as well.

Each of them is utterly absorbed in a heart-crushing journey—trudging along, slogging through. Listen:

   ∾ "Sir," sobs Mary Magdalene to the one she
      has good reason to suppose is the gardener,
      "if you have taken his body off somewhere,

tell me, please, so I can give him a decent burial myself."

～ "I won't believe till the impossible happens," Thomas bristles, brushing off the preposterous claim that Jesus is alive. Perhaps brushing back, as well, a haunting memory. "Let us go, that we may die with him," Thomas had said, as Jesus set his face toward the tomb of Lazarus. "I won't believe," says Thomas, reasonably enough, "until I see the marks of execution worn on a living body."

～ And Peter? Peter says, "I'm goin' fishin'!" (The man's got a way with words, doesn't he?)

Mary Magdalene, Thomas, and Peter—all three of them have an inkling that something strange has been going on, that this is not simply a case of Time's Up as usual. (Indeed, although the Gospel storyteller doesn't explicitly say so, there is reason to believe that Peter has already seen the Risen Christ when he announces his intention to head back to fishing.) Mary Magdalene, Thomas, and Peter—it sure does look like they are all just trying, in the midst of this heartbreak, to find some sort of closure. Wouldn't you be in search of the same?

So how does the Risen Christ deal with their Time's Up ideas about him, which, if he does not mercifully shatter, will be the death of them?

Watch closely. Do you see what Jesus does? He plays resurrection games with each of them. He pulls them in, head over heels, into rollicking, frolicking cartwheels of Divine Comedy.

Where did that come from, you reasonably ask? Let me try to explain, first by way of an anecdote.

A few years ago, my own rector was giving, to a standing-room-only crowd, a splendid sermon for Easter Sunday. Sitting with his parents was a little boy, maybe five or six, who had gotten up at the crack of dawn on Easter morning and gone in to find his overflowing Easter basket. (Can you blame him?) His parents weren't awake yet, so he decided to help himself to what he found. You can supply the next sentence, can't you? He ate the whole thing. He arrived for church utterly wired, on a sugar high to rival Mount Everest.

In the middle of her sermon, our priest uttered the single, seemingly incontrovertible, predictable, declaratory phrase: "This is Easter." At the top of his lungs, with total abandon, the little boy from his place in the pew spontaneously shrieked: "Yes it is!" The congregation, of course, broke into spontaneous laughter (just as you have done).

We were not laughing at him, were we? We were not putting him down, not a single one of us. We were joining in his joy. His "Yes, it is!" released our own.

At one level, what he said and did was out of place,

it didn't fit—but, at a deeper level, it was exactly what the whole day was all about. Our proper Episcopal expectations of Solemn Easter Joy came crashing down in waves of hilarious holy laughter.

I think the Jesus who cracked that temple whip now deals, in Amazing Grace, with his grieving followers by cracking splendid Easter jokes. Not jokes at their expense—but jokes into which they are invited, jokes in which their tears of hopeless anguish are transformed into tears of hopelessly hilarious joy.

～

"Tell me where you have taken him," sobs Mary Magdalene.

"Mary!" he says (you will have to fill in the tone of voice—it isn't in the text—but no matter how you hear it or say it, you have interpreted the story).

Mary looks and sees and clings for dear life.

"Mary," he says, "leggo my feet!" (That's not the original Greek, I grant you; but you won't escape the responsibility of playing in your own ear, as I am for you, the sound of "Do not hold on to me.")

You will remember that he let the other Mary anoint and wipe those feet—but that was before his death, and this is after his Resurrection.

"Hey, Mary Mag," I am hearing him say, "Touching is okay, just don't cling! Time isn't up; it's just getting started! Hey, my friend, you've no less days to sing God's praise than when you'd first begun."

∾

Thomas also wants a touch—a rather grosser kind of touch, frankly. Jesus says: "Okay, Tom, if that's what you really want—but wouldn't you really rather dance an 'I believe in resurrection' jig instead! [That's my loose translation of the original Greek.] After all, Thomas, you've no less days to sing God's praise than when you'd first begun."

∾

Peter—watch Peter closely. There he is, as such fishermen often are, "naked," "stripped for work." Someone calls from the beach. You know the story. Outrageous advice—an impossible catch—a sudden connection: "It's the Lord." What does he do?

Peter puts *on* his clothes, jumps in the water, and swims toward shore.

Ridiculous? At one level, surely.

But utterly understandable, in terms of how vulnerable he is—the denying disciple of a Risen Lord. So Peter drips his way through the first Easter breakfast buffet. Hilarious!

But now Jesus takes him aside for a private talk. Okay, the jig is up. There is no such thing as a free resurrection breakfast. Peter is in for a solemn reprimand, at least, probably a royal dressing down.

"Simon, do you love me"—once, twice, three times over—indirect rebuke for direct denial—time for time.

Jesus is really rubbing it in. Peter knows that he deserves every bit of what he's getting, though. But, oh my goodness, does this ever deeply hurt! Does Jesus *have* to rub it in like this?

But wait a minute, what, exactly *is* Peter getting a triple dose of?

Do you see what I see? A hint of a twinkle in Jesus' eye?

"Gotcha, Peter! Cut yourself some slack, fella. I already have. It was bad, I know. But I forgive you. We can share a laugh on the other side of that, can't we?" (How else do you know that somebody has really truly forgiven you unless at some point the two of you can laugh—not laugh it off, but laugh it through.)

"Hey, Peter, tag, you're it—now go feed my sheep, you hear? You've no less days to sing God's praise than when you'd first begun!"

~e~

Every idea we form of God, God must, in mercy, shatter—not smash, not pulverize, not grind into the dirt—but shatter, as in send exploding up in heavenly fireworks, one starburst after another.

Is that sheer speculation? I think not! Listen once more to the words from John's Gospel—right at the start, the author's clue to all the stories we have been listening to.

> In him was life, and the life was the light of all people. The light shines in the darkness, and the darkness did not overcome it. . . . The true light, which enlightens everyone, was coming into the world. . . . And the Word became flesh and lived among us, and we have seen his glory, . . . full of grace and truth. . . . From his fullness we have all received, grace upon grace. (1:4–16)

"Grace upon grace."

With grace like that, coming to us, pouring over us, each and all, again and again, what need have we to cling? For, after all, like all of his disciples in every age, we've no less days to sing God's praise than when we'd first begun.

Great and tender God: Draw us deeper and deeper into the shattering, shimmering joy of your Amazing Grace.

- *Steve France,* fellow parishioner at Redeemer, who read the draft, not once but twice, with a keen editor's eye—and provided the striking illustration offered in the first meditation.
- *The Rev. Dr. A. Katherine Grieb* and *Dr. Amy-Jill Levine,* passionate teachers, advocates for social justice, and New Testament scholars (at Virginia Theological Seminary and Vanderbilt Divinity School, respectively)—both of whom kindly read these imaginative adventures in Johannine theology with astute professional eyes. Dr. Levine in addition offered highly detailed and deeply insightful commentary, the influence of which infuses all of what you will shortly be reading.
- *Mr. Michael Wilt,* Editorial Director at Cowley Publications, who kept on believing that the publication of these meditations was, in fact, a good idea; and who has deftly overseen the editing and production process.
- *Dr. Margaret A. Tucker,* scientist, physician, healer, and housemate—the loving spouse whose support for her husband's homiletical freelancing is nothing short of amazing.

For over a decade I have also been graced by the friendship of *The Rev. Canon Russell Bowman-Eadie,* Director of Ministry Development in the Diocese of Bath and Wells, and Canon Treasurer in Wells Cathedral.

Russell is primarily responsible for initiating and nurturing my vocation as a regular preaching conference leader in the United Kingdom. No one plays a more central and crucial role in the formation of Church of England preachers, lay and ordained, than he.

More significant, Russell epitomizes homiletical imagination at its shimmering best: theology, poetry, music, drama, visual arts—all in constant creative synergy.

Since these "Amazing Grace" meditations are the closest approximation I can make to the theological artistry he embodies – – –

**This book is for Russell,
with gratitude and love.**

The Shattering Sound of Amazing Grace

Introduction

Comfortable Resonance and
Disorienting Dissonance

"Familiarity breeds contempt," the old adage runs.

True enough—but not the whole truth. This aphorism does what proverbs always do—it focuses attention on single features of a complex life canvas, where contrasting elements can prompt clashing maxims. ("Haste makes waste!" folks intone if we move too quickly. "He who hesitates is lost," they remind us if we don't move fast enough.) Familiarity sometimes breeds contempt—but it often leaves us feeling pretty comfortable.

The Gospel according to Saint John is a familiar text. The Jesus it portrays is widely recognized. John's Jesus (we well know) is a long-winded philosopher, a teacher who articulates lofty concepts in layers of circumlocutions. Jesus, for Saint John, is the Eternal *Logos* who seems out of place in the down-to-earth world where he comes to pitch his tent. Jesus, in the Fourth Gospel, is the Cosmic Sign-Spinner, tossing out "I AM" images, one upon another—Bread of Life, Living Water, True Vine, Good Shepherd. As portrayed in John's account of the Passion, Jesus is calm, collected, completely in charge—in sharp contrast to a harried Pilate, who scurries back and forth between the jeering crowd outside his palace and the regal prisoner who so intrudes on his interior space.

The Jesus of John—we know him: a mentor more mystical than the sometimes Aesop's Fable—sounding moral teacher that the Jesus of Matthew is made out to be. "We *don't* know the way!" protests Thomas in the Fourth Gospel, when Jesus says, matter-of-factly, "You know the way that I am going." A little later, after Jesus offers a bit more explanation, the disciples bravely say, "Now you are speaking plainly!" Those of us overhearing the conversation raise our eyebrows slightly ("Oh, *really!*"). But we aren't surprised; that's just how Jesus is in the Gospel of John.

The Johannine Jesus is decidedly more measured than the Jesus we find in the Gospel of Mark (in which he moves about so quickly, it's hard to keep track of him). John's Jesus shows no disposition to break into elaborate storytelling, as he does in Luke—he's too busy explaining and exhorting. He performs healings in John, as in the Synoptics, but he appears to employ those occasions primarily as object lessons, launching pads for his extended monologues.

Jesus in the Fourth Gospel is the one who proclaims (in John 3:16): *"For God so loved the world, that he gave his only begotten son, that whosoever believeth in him should not perish, but have everlasting life."* Odd words, perhaps, if you've never heard them—but reassuringly familiar to most of us, especially in the language of the King James Version. We know in advance what he's going to sound like—we've heard him so many times before.

But that is not how Jesus would have been perceived by the people he encounters in this Gospel. To these folks, Jesus is bewildering at best—"breath-taking" says it better. The worlds of those whom Jesus comes upon are invaded, upended, shattered—time and again. The Jesus with whom they must come to terms is not at all familiar.

ꝏ

"Familiarity breeds not contempt but comfort"—you could say the same of "Amazing Grace"—"that great old hymn of the faith," a song universally known and loved irrespective of one's religious affiliation. "Amazing Grace" is played and sung in all sorts of places, not just churches. It is, as it were, the "comfort food" of Christian hymnody. It is widely tolerated, even appreciated by many "who don't believe a word of it." Familiarity works that way.

In the following pages, I propose to interplay these two familiarities, the Jesus of John's Gospel and the hymn "Amazing Grace," hoping that a certain fresh resonance between the two will sharpen the disorienting dissonance that, beneath familiar phrases, permeates each one. At the heart of this text, and this tune, lies a truth succinctly articulated by C. S. Lewis in a proverb—perhaps the only one I know that tells the whole truth: "Every idea of God we form, God must, in mercy, shatter."

1

Drink to Love, Don't Try to Sell It!

Jaded Palates and Cleansing Wine

JOHN 2:1–21

> Amazing grace! How sweet the sound that
> saved a wretch like me.
> I once was lost, but now am found; was blind,
> but now I see.

Amazing grace, how sweet the sound! The tune is so familiar it all but hums itself. The lines have washed over us so many times, we probably know them by heart, even if we've never sat down to memorize them.

Growing up as a preacher's kid, I did a lot of time in church. There were abundant occasions for boyhood boredom. Long sermons, prayers, announcements—it felt like I was serving a prison sentence. Music didn't often help; yet, I never got tired of singing "Amazing Grace." Something transfixed the atmosphere when the congregation commenced that hymn. Eyes glistened, faces glowed. The room warmed up, took on a rosy hue. Breaking spontaneously into four-part harmony, the entire assembly became a choir. God—however hard to access through seemingly endless spoken words—suddenly seemed to come down close when everyone sang "Amazing Grace." Chills charged up and down my spine. A glance across the room assured me that mine wasn't the only spine tingling. Singing "Amazing Grace" as a youngster conjured up the sense of community one feels when roasting marshmallows with best friends around a blazing campfire—"This is wonderful! Can we just keep doing it all night long?"

So—it was rather disconcerting for me, one day well into middle age, to come upon the text of this hymn in bald print: words with no notes, sentences with no music. "Amazing grace, how sweet the sound." What in the world could that possibly mean?

What is *grace* (besides a woman's first name)? What's so *amazing* about it? What is the *sound* of *amazing,* and what makes that sound *sweet?* One upon another, questions tumbled in. Too many for quick and easy answering—plenty to ponder and reflect upon.

        ᴄ "How *sweet* the sound . . ."

                › "Sweet" like Muzak in a shopping
                   mall? Like the sweep of violins on a

romantic evening, complementing candlelight and wine?

› Is Amazing Grace "sweet" like the clear, happy voice of an exuberant child: "Mommy, you're the best!"?

› Or might the sound of "sweet" in Amazing Grace be closer to the piercing wail of Scottish bagpipes at the funeral of a New York fireman—loosening stiff upper lips, dissolving dams of firm resolve into floods of tears?

› My friend Stephen France told me something he once read: A man long incarcerated in a German prisoner-of-war camp said, after his release, that the sweetest sound he ever heard was the grinding of tank treads as Allied forces arrived to liberate him and his colleagues from Dachau. Is *that* the "sweet sound" of Amazing Grace?

꘎ "How sweet the *sound* . . .": Apart from being "sweet," what might it mean for grace to "sound" at all? How does one recognize it when one hears it?

› Is the sound of grace a gentle rustling, like wind whispering in the trees?

> A rollicking, frolicking sound, like a rushing mountain stream in the middle of a forest?

> A plainsong chant swirling through the chapel of a monastery?

But could grace, in fact, have a whole spectrum of sounds to play?

> Could it sometimes sound annoying—like the harsh, rude blare of a honking horn?

> Alarming, like the howl of an approaching siren?

> Startling, like the crack and boom of sudden thunder?

~ "*Amazing* grace, how sweet the sound": What makes grace "amazing"?

> That it comes as an unexpected bolt of good fortune—like a ten million-dollar door knock from the Prize Patrol at Publisher's Clearing House?

> That it's the mesmerizing manifestation of an extraordinary feat of skill—the high shimmering note of a virtuoso soprano, hanging in the air for what seems like forever? An impossibly acrobatic catch by the center fielder, robbing the long-ball hitter of his home run?

On the other hand:

> › Could "amazing" ever be encountered as the shock of an unexpected phone call: "Your job has been terminated. Clean out your desk and leave the building within an hour."

> › Might "amazing" mean the appearing of what you had given up all hope of hearing—the words "I forgive you," spoken by someone whose voice you never expected to hear again?

~ "Amazing *grace* . . ."

Well, what is it, actually?

> › Dazzling charm?

> › Abundant kindness?

> › "Unmerited favor" is the definition I remember coming upon long ago, ensconced in a theological dictionary. (It didn't shed a lot of light when I first encountered it, and it strikes me still as rather like explaining the obscure in terms of the unintelligible.)

Amazing grace, how sweet the sound—How could I have understood so little of what I thought I knew so well? The longer I sifted through the old kit bag of my "Amazing Grace" associations, the more apparent it became that I had not traveled all that far from another boyhood image: grace as the last big present under the Christmas tree—the one hoped for (and secretly expected), the one about which, upon opening, you proclaim with prerehearsed delight: "Wow! Just what I've always wanted!" How does that notion of Amazing Grace get translated into the world of one who has supposedly grown up?

- ~ A big fat check from Rich Uncle God (whether resources to be drawn upon are material or spiritual)?
- ~ A "get out of jail free" card in the game of Religious Monopoly?
- ~ A welcome respite in the midst of a dry spiritual routine or a protracted desert journey ("God, I'm bored, burned out—if you would, please, just amaze me with some grace")?

Amazing Grace, it became apparent, was altogether too familiar—and familiarity had bred within me a certain conscious comfort, and an unconscious contempt as well.

I suspect, however, that the people who encounter Jesus in the Gospel according to John would never be tempted in the slightest to regard the sweet sound of Amazing Grace as "the sound of sweet nothings in your ear":

- Those in attendance at the wedding in Cana
- Those standing in the temple courtyard as he drove out animal sellers and money changers
- A Pharisee named Nicodemus, a leader of the Jews
- A Samaritan woman, on a trip to the well
- A woman caught in adultery
- A man born blind
- Two sisters, Mary and Martha, devastated at the death of brother Lazarus

The spontaneous reactions of all these, upon encountering "grace" in the words and actions of Jesus, I wager, would probably sound something like: "What in God's name was that! Where in the world did it come from? Who let it loose in my life, and why? However it got here, could I please send it back?"

Asked about the meaning of Amazing Grace, I'm guessing that the responses of those assailed by it in John's Gospel would be anything but sentimental: "Grace? I'll tell you about grace! Grace is the world as one knows it torn apart, and reconfigured almost beyond recognition! Grace turns you inside out and upside down. It takes your breath and leaves you gasping."

It is, of course, impossible for us to climb inside the heads of characters caught up in the Grace-incursions described by the author of the Fourth Gospel. But the interactions this writer depicts are of such high energy that it will not do for us to treat these dramas as dispensable "illustrations" of some "main point." These intense Amazing Grace dramas, rather than any theological abstractions extruded from them, are the heart of a Gospel that commences with the claim: "The Word became flesh and lived among us."

Flesh *feels*. To set those feelings on a shelf while attempting to describe and interpret what happens for humanity when Word informs flesh—well—that is to render the impact of sound, sense, and personal interaction as though these were only illustrations of disembodied ideas; and that doesn't much sound like an "Incarnate Word." The heart of the Gospel that tradition names "John" is a Gospel that *touches* hearts. And it leaves them, by turns, fluttering, racing, pounding, skipping—very often stopped cold, frozen in fear. The stories of those who meet Jesus in the Gospel of John are, in a sense, tales of Holy Terror.

Playing out the action settings of the folks who encounter Amazing Grace in John's Gospel inevitably requires imagination. That is fraught with risk, admittedly.

Such a risk is like the one that any conductor must take with a musical score, the risk of shouldering responsibility for rendering a composer's mind and meaning with appropriate expression, appropriate feeling. The composer's own notes and markings must be honored, certainly—but those can only stimulate (and never substitute for) a conductor's interpretive expression. So it is with drama producers and preachers. There is no other way to be deeply faithful to a score, a script, a text than to interpret it with as much responsible creativity as one can summon.

What might it mean, traveling alongside folks who stumble upon it in John's Gospel, to savor the sound of Amazing Grace? Let us see and smell—taste and touch—and listen.

There was a wedding in Cana of Galilee, and the mother of Jesus was there. Jesus and his disciples had also been invited to the wedding. When the wine gave out, the mother of Jesus said to him, "They have no wine." And Jesus said to her, "Woman, what concern is that to you and to me? My hour has not yet come." His mother said to the servants, "Do whatever he tells you." Now standing there were six stone water jars for the Jewish rites of purification, each holding twenty or thirty gallons.

Jesus said to them, "Fill the jars with water."
And they filled them up to the brim. He said to
them, "Now draw some out, and take it to the
chief steward." So they took it. When the steward tasted the water that had become wine, and
did not know where it came from (though the
servants who had drawn the water knew), the
steward called the bridegroom and said to him,
"Everyone serves the good wine first, and then
the inferior wine after the guests have become
drunk. But you have kept the good wine until
now." (2:1–10)

The Passover of the Jews was near, and Jesus
went up to Jerusalem. In the temple he found
people selling cattle, sheep, and doves, and the
money changers seated at their tables. Making
a whip of cords, he drove all of them out of
the temple, both the sheep and the cattle. He
also poured out the coins of the money changers and overturned their tables. He told those
who were selling the doves, "Take these things
out of here! Stop making my Father's house a
marketplace!" (2:13–16)

Two sudden incursions, lightning strikes almost—
one following close upon the other (only days apart,